DINOSAUR DREAMS

By Troy Graham

Copyright © 2023 By Troy Graham

No portion of this publication may be reproduced or transmitted in any form, or by any means, without the express written permission of the copyright holders. Names, characters, places and incidents featured in this publication either are the product of the author's imagination or are used fictitiously. Any resemblance to actual persons living or dead is entirely coincidental.

All rights reserved.
Cover art and book design by Lisa Graham
Dinosaur images by Shawn Wolfman
(Original artwork from music posters)

Special thanks to Marty Achatz for being an inspiration to me.

MORNING

Here I stand on a cold, windy morning
It's mid-November and the world is silent for now
Fresh snow on the ground, the trees are bare

As I watch a crow do a brilliant dance in the snow
I think to myself, how did we all get here?

Inflation is so high that almost no one can afford to live
Most people who survived the pandemic
are not kind to each other anymore.

That is where humans have ended up
Silently coexisting with as few words as possible
The world only communicates through screens these days

Something is very wrong
I can't take it anymore, all of the hate
depression, so many people impatient
with nothing good to say

The way the world is now, is why I live
under the strict belief that all of us
are nothing more than the subconscious dreams of
dinosaurs and our world will end when they awake from
their soft slumber

So the next time you get a chance to go outside
and breath the cold frosty air
be grateful that the dinosaurs have not yet woken up
Hope that they will keep dreaming away

Because once they wake up, we will just be a thought
and we will have no more windy winter days

LULLABY OF THE TREES

Looking in my rear view mirror, seeing
your house get smaller and smaller

I can hear the lullaby of the trees as I'm
driving down your road on a crisp autumn night

There is not much in front of me that I can see
All I can hear is the lullaby of the trees
as they are blowing in the wind

I hear the trees before the day even begins
as they are covered in snow

Turns out the lullaby of the trees is the only
love song I know

RAIN DROP MARY

They called her Raindrop Mary
because every time she would cry, it would rain
hard for days and days

Time stood still
to feel her pain

The copper colored pigeon is her only friend
She gave up on people long ago because she could
not seem to find good humans anymore

So now most of her sorrow takes place behind
a closed, locked door

A quiet room is the only place
she feels safe

They call her Raindrop Mary now watch
as all of her tears go straight down the drain

SLEEPING BAG

A place I would go as a kid when I was sad
My own imaginary world
with soft walls, soft sides that smell like popcorn
The place where I felt most understood
where all my dreams came true
where I felt safe
Time was irrelevant
Nothing mattered except
what I believed

As a kid my favorite place was my sleeping bag

Ok your turn to share

THE MOTH AND THE MOON

The moth and the moon dance together
on a cold pale afternoon

As earth orbits sun
the moon reminds me of you

Elegant strong bright and true
The way your eyes glow in the night sky

I am like the moth
Drifting aimlessly
And then you save me
from the unforgiving sky

I'm still learning
How to fly
floating in the air
like a slightly deflated balloon

I am the moth
You are the moon

HOLLOW

Day dreams are real
When you are dead

The bird froze to death
in December sitting in a tree

Fade into the shadows
so your pain can no longer be seen

The closer you get to autumn
the smaller your shadow becomes

Soon there will be no place to hide

maybe the frozen bird's last thought
was where did things go wrong

Reading books to be one
with the world and politics
shows me nothing but defeat

There is no sign of shore
and the water is rising beneath my feet

Daydreams are real when you're dead
So pay no attention to those voices inside your head

UNCONDITIONAL LOVE

A lot of people throughout my life have asked me
what I think unconditional love is
My answer is simple

Unconditional love is a bath mat you put inside your tub
It's there when you don't notice it
when you have forgotten about it
when you step all over it

So even though you put it through hell
treat it like trash
It's there
making sure you don't fall

DISMAL NIGHT

See each drop of rain
Dripping from the windchime
That hangs off my back porch

Walking down the fire escape
In mid-February for no reason at all
Each slab of wood I walk on sings its own song

13 dollars in my pocket and wool socks on my feet
I cut through the backlot of my neighbor's yard
and reach the street

Looking left to right right to left
Not a car or a person in sight
I'm alone as I walk this cold yet dismal night

Watching the snow banks getting
taller each day
I wonder when the winter night will hear what I say

The February fog and snow plows are my only friends
At 4 a.m.

I'm not looking for a new beginning
just wondering where this all will end

HEADSTONE

Here I sit in the cemetery
at 2 a.m. drunk as the night is long
There's a ketchup bottle on the headstone
that I'm leaning on

I wish I had better words for this situation
or maybe even a song
Here I lie looking at the spinning stars
wondering where I went wrong

How did the ketchup bottle get here
I'll never know
It's pretty cold in the cemetery in December
when you're sitting in snow

DEAD LEAVES

All of the dead leaves
soft as silk on the ground

All of the dead leaves
tormented by the wind spin round and round

All the dead leaves so beautiful,
they make life worth living
In this unforgiving world

There is meaning behind all the leaves, alive or dead
For every boy, every girl

CROW IN THE SNOW

Sometimes when I wake up drenched
in sweat and feel that nightmare shiver

I think of a crow in the snow

Sometimes when I can't hear anything
Except nothingness
And the sound of screaming people
Inside the walls

I think of a crow in the snow

When I think of the dead flowers
Lying on his grave and the last memory
I have of when he was still alive

I think of the crow in the snow

When I look back on my life
It's hard to say where I've been or should go

Each and every day I find
Myself thinking

of the crow in the snow

PANCAKES

John liked pancakes
Tess liked french toast

They got married when they were just 18 years old
The years passed like water down a drain

Things didn't work out, they were
Riding different trains

As the moon rose, the sun went down
Tess said to John I guess I'lll see you 'round

They should have seen they were too different
When John said he liked pancakes

And Tess said she liked french toast

A WINTER'S POEM

Where are you, humanity?
Are you somewhere between the flowers?
Or somewhere between the trees?

Are we all nothing more than anger,
Or some long-lasting disease?

I once saw people be kind, but now that's all gone
So keep your mask up, keep your distance
Wait for the next thing to go wrong

Or change with the day, shift with the tide
If we all learn to love again, we don't need to run, hide

People are fragile, often don't know what to do
If we can all learn to love again
I believe everything will be new

99

99 neatly-knitted scarves wrapped around the
necks of newly nautical men

99 ghosts waiting for the world to say when
can you come back to the place where you dwelled

99 half-hearted souls, stranded in hell
99 wives cling to their husbands' farewells

Wives say goodbye to their men
As they are going to sea

99 neatly-knitted scarves wrapped around the
necks of newly-nautical men and me

THE LEAVES WILL FALL
AS THEY MAY

With your shotgun and your bible
You preach the devils dance recital
And I'm strung out on tomorrow but there is still today

Looking right to left left to right
Nothing to say
We can't predict what is to come
The leaves will fall as they may

Money rules all, the naive, weak, and cruel
the corporations and some of you, too
So the leaves will fall as they may

On a gray pale afternoon
I see the sidewalk beneath my shoes
can't tell what is true

The leaves will fall as they may

SILHOUETTE IN THE WINDOW

The silhouette in the window zeroes her to the bone
It's the silhouette in the window
That won't leave her alone

The silhouette in the window is dark and cold
It's the silhouette in the window that makes her old

The silhouette in the window has done something wrong
But can't say it out loud

She asked the silhouette in the window
What are your secrets? Who else knows?
The silhouette in the window in a spider voice
Says just us for now

(For the cast and crew of just us for now)

ARE WE THERE YET?

How do you baptize someone when they are in hell?
So many cigarettes in the ashtray

Darling, are we there yet?
Where? you ask

Somewhere that the wind swallows the tide in sweet
December, or somewhere between the look in your
eyes when I tell you I'm leaving again

Darling, are we there yet?
Where? you ask

Somewhere between the parting clouds
Or the half naked trees in autumn
And somewhere between your heart and mine

Darling, are we there yet?

Are we forgotten like the chalk drawing of children
Playing in front of a liquor store before the rain comes?
Are we forgotten like a painter who killed herself
Before her masterpiece was ever painted?

Darling,are we there yet?
And I answer, yes. We are just where we need to be no
more, no less

BIRTHDAY

The child came into this world
Soft as his mother's palm
Naked as the evening sky
after a late autumn storm

The first thing the child saw was
the hope in his father's eyes

There is no pain
No confusion, only
His mother's love, father's joy

On this 27th of April
Your parents celebrate
this blessing this gift
Their sweet baby boy

For Carter

CHEERS TO YOU

Cheers to you, my dear Aunt Cathy
Because now you are an angel in the sky

I'll have a cheers for you my dear Aunt Cathy
on Nov 15, 2022, the day you died

Cheers to all the good memories I have
Not all the time when you were in pain

It is you Aunt Cathy in each little drop of rain
You in that better place

Yet I will miss you each day

Oh my dear Aunt Cathy I know your
spirit will light my way

(Cheers to you. You will be deeply missed)

APPLE TREE

So many apples hang from the tree
Some are different, some are a lot like me

From man to woman
Boy to girl
Earth to sea
There are so many
apples hanging from the tree

I wish for people to have no judgment
for there to be no space between
you and me

We are all different apples
hanging from the same tree

Close your eyes take a deep breath
Now exhale
You are free

THE POET

The poet sits hunched over in the chair
His blue eyes tremble as a cigarette
Burns through his fingers

Where did all the years go?

All the lovers, parties, all the friends long gone
The poet is growing old
but believes he has one last song

One more group of words before he goes
to make his coffin warm

One more group of words to make the world
less dark and torn

One last group of words before he dances
with stars in the sky

One more group of words to leave less
people wondering why

MEET THE AUTHOR

TROY GRAHAM is a poet, and folk musician from Marquette, MI. His passion is writing music and poems and engaging with youth through special workshops and events. In the summers, you will find him touring throughout the Great Lakes region sharing his love of words and melody.